THE
YEAR
OF THE
ROOSTER

AHSAHTA PRESS
BOISE, IDAHO
2013

THE NEW SERIES
#54

THE
YEAR
OF THE
ROOSTER

NOAH ELI GORDON

Ahsahta Press, Boise State University, Boise, Idaho 83725-1525
ahsahtapress.org
Cover design by HR Hegnauer
Cover artwork: "God meets w/Satan," Jon Read, 2007, acrylic, glitter, on paper.
Book design by Janet Holmes
Printed in Canada

LIBRARY OF CONGRESS CATALOGING-IN-PUBLICATION DATA

Gordon, Noah Eli, 1975-
The Year of the Rooster / Noah Eli Gordon.
pages cm. -- (The New Series ; #54)
ISBN-13: 978-1-934103-40-1 (pbk. : alk. paper)
ISBN-10: 1-934103-40-3 (pbk. : alk. paper)
I. Title.
PS3607.O5943Y43 2013
811'.6--DC23
2013000577

in memory of

JAKE ADAM YORK

August 10, 1972 – December 16, 2012

Thank you for listening attentively when I read aloud on the way from Denver to Lincoln the lengthy title poem here. Thank you for your ear, for your heart, for your hand. It was freezing that day and the next. You were always warm, vehement, benevolent.

cutting an elsewhere
in the air

CONTENTS

DIMINISHING
RETURNS

ALL ORANGE BLOSSOMS HAVE TO DO
IS ACT NATURALLY

& all the sky does is wait around for weather to consume it.
Although, one could argue that it's simply an extension of itself,
that one form describes another in the sails of outrigger canoes
before a landward breeze blows them toward the Philippine coast.

If I stand still long enough, the painting will go on without me.
Forget the mechanics of rainfall; Plutarch said it was war caused
a cloudburst. I say the only thing in the air is an evolving suspicion
that the laws of the atmosphere have accumulated out of a desire

to turn judiciousness on top of its Draconian head, reclaiming
sound judgment from the silver gavel affixed to our internalized sense
of fanciful reasoning taken for fact. All Galileo does is build a thermometer
& immediately—you believe him. Trade winds & doldrums in the tropics.

Delicate mobility in the deer. I love the tiny molecules that make up matter,
the tinier atoms inside them. If I stand still long enough, someone will walk around me.

A PAINTING OF A STILL DEER
IS A MOVING ARGUMENT
FROM MULTIPLE PERSPECTIVES

I refuse to explain this. Instead, consider the foreground, blunted
by an excess of brownish pigment, meant, as one immediately discerns,
to resemble the forest floor covered in fallen pine needles, & how it is
here that the nature of dramatic illusion is not so much on display

as it *is* display, while the illusion of dramatic nature frees one to embrace
an indifference for the animal. During the intervening successive moments, I've
decided to exclude myself from the conversation, as it too is in its entirety
a single instant in which I've already moved on. Here's me heading back,

turning toward the house. & here, the red ceramic tea kettle, the one with a large
chip in its handle. I've always harbored an eccentric interest in broken objects.
Often one hears of a work of art as having been ruined, but never broken. Leaving
aside the deer, which has, like us, moved on, at least we can agree on one thing:

logic requires some foundation in sense. I have an inkling of where it's off to.

A LEAP FROM THE ATMOSPHERE
OF SCHOLARSHIP

Projected on the wall, an essentialist's idiot order becomes the wall,
becoming itself a projector through which one might animate a door
swinging between open & concealed eroticism. At seventeen, Schubert
gives Gretchen her grave. At thirty, who isn't a melancholy antihero

haunting French literature? Pitched one octave below the oboe, pinned
to transparent paper, sentimental as an anecdote driven toward self-deification,
the empire of systemically expressed thought dusts its lilies. I'm convinced
that covering a chameleon in ink would cancel natural phenomena.

Turning the conviction timeless, unmoving, & immutable, an arrow passes
our illusion—a long exile from one's own blackened sheep. The worm
at home in its blindness. The inelastic world latched up. Modern evolutionary
scientists no longer search for the missing link. Nevertheless, it does move.

WHEN THE ATMOSPHERE
IN THE OPERA HOUSE IS AGAINST YOU

Just walk out. Some advice is effective in its obviousness.
Among a cheering crowd, one looks not for the source of its jubilance,
but for how one might approach it. Meanwhile, the singing has stopped.
If a tree free from its landscape no longer reflects the harmony

of the universe, then what is one to do with so many jettisoned ideas
for uprooting received notions of a novice painter's proper subjects?
I could watch clouds for hours, but that doesn't make me interesting.
The stage is a metaphor for the stage. The crowd is a guard against advice.

Turning immediately to the end of a book reveals nothing except
one's willful rejection of what might have been, finally, an ill-conceived plan.
Yet there was purpose in it. I think I'll call this: "The auditorium is now empty"

ARE YOU ASHAMED OF THE INDIFFERENCE WITH WHICH YOU GREET THE NEWS OF THE DEATH OF PINOCHET

Lyrically, country & western music is a combination of the trials
& successes of everyday life. Gilbert & Sullivan are a combination,
but the satirizing of society of the Victorian period hardly seems relevant
to our present concern. Pitched lower than a trumpet & higher than a tuba,

the French horn is not a combination. What, exactly, is fearful symmetry?
The two largest individual optical telescopes on Earth sitting atop Mauna Kea?
Thousands of small photographs combining to form the image of a wolf?
An object held in one's hand having potential energy, a combination

turning motion, position, & mass into a balanced definition? I've never held
a French horn, but think I would enjoy the equilibrium of its potential heft.

WHERE IS THE PIANO I LIVED MY LIFE ON

Or where is my life outside of pianos? A hammer strikes its string & Lear
jumps again into regret. Glorious to leave a kitchen & glorious to live only
for kitchens & glorious to enter unexpected an igloo aglow in embers
& glorious to lay out in the usual rigid Roman grid pattern & glorious

to balance in one's palm the perfect sandwich & glorious the substance
& the accident & everything underneath. A shadow moves across the wall
& I see a shadow moving across this wall. Laughter at the far end of
impersonality, a crutch for freestanding facts. Luck in its burgeoning form

turns rational experience, like a buckeye rolling toward you, away from itself.

A PROPOSAL AS ARBITRARY AS THE PHENOMENA IT PURPORTS TO ELIMINATE

Pivot the linguistics encyclopedia, & allocations covering a lead moth, idle
in the air above its impropriety, land like a Meet-Your-Waterloo-Here placard
just outside of the pristine convention hall. Landscape was never something
capacious you could up & walk in. One foot bobbing in the buoyant negation,

the other on firm old ground following perspective. If I were a sculptor, this
model would be clear as quotation: to begin pick anything from the book of
best-selling plots. Dear Lolita, Dear Lesbia, a towering figure of the 20th century,
trapped in a sexual lexicon, declares the rose in love with its wooden box.

THE FIRST PROMINENT SYMBOL INTONES SUGGESTIONS FOR FURTHER READING

There's nothing like the present, like the president, like a precedent leaking
in analog its continuous signal. Life on Capitol Hill is calamitous! cries the paper.
Torn to pieces, tossed into the Nile, voted most likely to forget music, all news
like a blind dervish in the doorway tuning one's attention. Neon light littering

our film noir in white music behind a blue naturalist's gray voiceover. Too many
ideas destroy the image as always, & sickly from birth Hildegard von Bingen
calls you a cross within the world or the world is your careless happy cross.

OBLITERATING HISTORY IN THE PLEASURE
OF HOLDING FORTH

A first line is reason enough for a second, for a segment, unisexual & solitary as an organ. Our doctor operates a mechanism & calls it anatomy. Our dancer operates in music, which is the same. Whorled, lance-shaped leaves smear the window. Windy instrument, windy agency. Active principles everywhere

charging inertia. Syntactic propositions rest a harmonious unified totality on a reupholstered couch. Smash the shell to bits & hear the ocean in this lime.

HOLD TOGETHER WITH A STITCH
THE WHOLE OF CAUSALITY

I could have been a contender, or, tender as a helicopter, I could have set
afloat adrift this bed & its contortive aspirations, moving all afternoon
between black & white music. You turn to the dictionary of literary terms
by mistake. Relative bodies, resting bodies, entire arms erased. A metronome

calls out colorless death to any future metaphysicians in our digital world.

THE POEM & POST-IT NOTE ARE ONE

The most decadent numeral, alive as a nominalist running all week through black grass, all weekend through blown-out examples of the corrupt material world: bus systems, library systems, systemic encounters with physical objects toppling the ideal city's infrastructure. Two by two, animals fall from the acropolis.

THE GRAMMAR OF ARCHITECTURE
IS ONLY A BOOK

Begin with the pale fox I would for you bathe in brittle iris leaves. It's easy to grant a small creature love. Now, return to your tiny paper house a little darkness raising its sail, Orphic insight as a modern slot machine's explanation of itself.

IF IT'S OUR LOT TO EXPAND
THE DOLPHIN SO BE IT!

Happiness was never a swan cast in concrete, a life whittled down by negation, then expanded by German philosophy. On earth, privilege the position of earth.

A SUBJECTIVE MATTER

A compost for vivid & evocative description decomposes ruinously its nostalgia.

THE
YEAR
OF THE
ROOSTER

He's wearing both a dress and pants

ALICE NOTLEY

A woman I mix men up

BERNADETTE MAYER

He had only the accidental pictorial interest in mind

PHILIP WHALEN

Morning orchestrates its little engines—

residual truth, frightening rain, a leaf
shaking with yellow jacket liftoff

It's a deafening sound drives through
sincerity, its armored trees & sad insects

Who'd want to move from the particular?

Clouds shape themselves judiciously

go to ghost windows
                    I've lived every new city in
So programmatic & unsunned

                    // oil inertia //
        // honey inertia //
            // nerve endings & string //

An accomplice to thirst is gracious

Bind & link the Rooster thinking
a protracted present can't keep the characters straight

Cliff-Noted Infamous Death

Sun Making a Color Wheel of Oil Spots

There were dragonflies over the pond

Like the Rooster puts words behind my eyes
& calls it more a mouth than speaking would

Does this window have a name?

                                    Yes

Will you sing it?

                        Hush me

He doesn't

believe

in the farm

that he's sure

he must have

thought into

being

but believes

in the thought

being

farm-like

& thinks

everything else

unnecessary

Is dawn's
willing spokesman

espousing himself
in half-light

or is it
the light's

half solicited
by his simple rhetoric?

"SomeThing SomeThing"

I think, slipping to the floor

A burning twig's a small fire

Hello, another Edison idea

Thought vaccine

Thought collapse

Before I died I was a thief now I'm a head of state bored of full talking

Death's a touch-me-not trigger
constellates around the Rooster

Apologetic penis, don't try to make me
one of your machines

Who said it?

Him or me?

If suffering pronouns are only words
I must be a ghost of it

Something else to weld evening together

A few distant footfalls, dominant oblivion

This muffled practice stunning as a binder clip
makes the best furniture for adjectival distance

WELCOME TO THE YEAR OF THE ROO

Bantam hypothesis: history's gone a half step into human verbs

Gutted architecture, global compliance

The first to the finish line is always first to the finish line

Gratuitous self-perpetuating publicity

Eight weeks in broken collarbone
& aesthetic tendencies instead of ideas

Proof that one's voice at very least is wanting
contact, has a pedestrian flair

I dream
　　a stage
　　　　& stand on it
　　　　ontological as any
　　　fare-thee-well deed
of separation

Endurance is
　　daily fulminating
　　　　animistic otherness

　　　　　Explain thyself
　　　　　& expunge
　　　　　　cape-&-gown aerobatics
　　　　　　elevating the sudden
　　　　　　　manifestation of
　　　　　　　essential truth
　　　　　　　　into a one-size-
　　　　　　　　fits-all expression

Why should I be clear facing convoluted ethos?

Moderate passion
    never pushed one to master
      the noose, to practice scales
        across scalding keys, weathering
          hothouse vigor with heavy grade
        weld-mesh wire around the
      henhouse's penning in
        of perpetual adoration

A biting monologue begins by keeping your mouth shut

Vastness is what
        Roo reclines into, an electric moon
    & all its circumferential distance

How many feet marking how far they
    have to march to call it a parade

The moon does the same small dance
    over & over & it's a wonder he let me
dig my claws this far into the dark,
    though I can't tell if he's me & I'm
something else the Rooster wants
    emerging, bound to anthropological
endearment

She laughs when I say the Rooster's dead

Maiden with Mirror
is that behemoth that is

Honing it to a dot, the logistics
to dismantling a loophole

You have something to say, why not say it?

It's nothing

They gave me a trumpet & I think of the movies
& loneliness like a bottled-up doubt

Ice on the lake

Did you mean lacking?

I'm not talking I am

After details, everything quaking
A history (if that's the word) being opened
You don't share a house you share
rooms, feathers, an even memory's wake-up call

It's stagnant
but the Rooster's a trope, regal
without subordination & attendant baggage

Even wasps have feathers

No, too skinny

Everything skinny is ominous

Electro-legged spider crosses the page
           patterns a field patterned by need
           fielding its urgency into another trade-off

Condensed captive phenomena
triggering vacant description
as if wallpaper were a starting point
or martyrdom a made-up word

Is there no art ascribed to eating?
Is this eating a reverence
for original noise? Stunning reception hour?

I swear disasters happen everywhere

        Meaningless day
               split in two

          spurring nothing

Fuck if I launch my little boat

Would you call that a trumpet I would

She wants a microscope & if it's science then
there's no music just talking words

I dream alarmed a lot

You're not presenting an idea; you're stating a problem

I have a spear

Nomadic inertia pitching a tent
Inside, internationality picks up
after itself little pieces of Rooster-thought

How far can you throw your spear?

I have a spear

Dressed in grammar
clamorous as a walk-on's
wish for a few words
a deadening idea
marries itself
to whatever I've been
trying to get across:

          fields, farms, the faraway certainty
              of affection for ritualized work
            when work's a camera-less close-up
          of everything I couldn't bother to include

        I dream a stage
          & stand on it

Countess
colonizer
   who else
strolls on
   a ridge of
holly & calls
   it difficult
to imagine
   a more
decorative
   holiday?

I don't want
my time off, want
to live deliberate, a wife
to each pretty picture
of finality they've pasted
inside of me

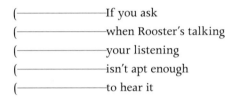

(————————If you ask
(————————when Rooster's talking
(————————your listening
(————————isn't apt enough
(————————to hear it

A personal condemnation
collects its dust
like all good statues
but who's molded us
into the pronoun we're after?

Propped in the courtyard &
covered by sun
a wobbly, gleeful god
expansive as a spotlight
agitating for more amplification

Trick's no longer to photograph the bullet:
accelerated escapism rearviewed irony ages ago

I'll atone for the orbit I'm in
for an inked hourglass, stupid sandcastle

O indoors you do me in so delicious, a week's worth of nature shows
showing nothing of light catching our animals triumphantly ignoring us

Am I seeding or sunning myself, forfeiting
a manual of dignities to feign composure?

Collecting discharge decomposition carries
dangling a carrot in front of a theoretical mule
something akin to startup fervor, sweat & its saltlick altar
ominous rust on an ice pick, the impromptu ballet in a palmist's index finger
tracing a line I might as well rely on

Good Good dawning Rooster

Even statues lean into source material
A little less reverb on the veranda

Ha!

Rooster says that kind of routine letdown gets somewhere

Only thing I can't tell is the starting point from the part already lost

A dead ringer for slim familiarity, a stranger
seen a half dozen times in a single day

Now, wind knocks its way past window ruts

Dramatic logics of a lone blue jay
beat against the back of my neck
& afternoon's airing its pertinent grievances

How dim these cigarettes seem
when geometric patterns of the rug keep me occupied
until the dinner bell rings its egalitarian yes to a ruined offering

Sure I carry my nobility like a mule can't sustain a human agenda

Dream a stage & stand on it

Dream a page from the Book of Perfect Beginnings & claw it to confetti

Dream a hearse & crash it into the hospital

Dream yourself inside the egg
    inside the syringe's sterility
        inside a mannequin & then take off its clothes

Dream like an animal
  in gray tones, like a mammal
  in motherliness, in public
    dream as purposeful as possible
      put on whatever's laid out
        & wedge yourself between
          waning fashion & a wonderful tan

Are you a photographer of staged mutations?

Yes, thank you

Would you take rust on that blue Volkswagen roadside as a conceit?

Yes, thank you

Draw a mannequin across the tile floor until one of its legs comes loose?

Yes, thank you

Call this momentary withdrawal a series
of equations which thinking a perimeter makes?

Yes & thank you
amid hurried blurs
the day's become
a mound of snow
graying in the center
of an otherwise vacant lot

Two seasons later
it's the shell of a beetle
baking in the sun

brittle in the sun

I watch over you because you need me

Forgive the systematic contortion
of removals, from a coarseness comes
a fiery magnetism, from an anxious dream
an encroaching boredom

After four hours
dawdling with the wardrobe, I leave furiously
a city & its wintering sheen, remove
the hens, then those for whom
the remaining space is responsible

Commodify me
a pretty mess conjugation
  Three shafts of grass
     wanting notice
          or noticing what
       afternoon light
          charges, exchanging
                attentiveness
          for dustbin
       representations
    of dull mulchings
                civility makes

Receding coastline, judicial waistline
       Commercial fallout
             battering the braincase
          builds a husk
       around actual things
          between you & me
    am I thinking this
          fencepost this
             flowerpot that
          sad red bird

Decorous passivity binds me to the drawing room
Wait an hour or two & Roo appears

It's easy to erase him
tending landscapes a rusting battery accentuates

A smidge of ambition
becomes the wail of passing planes

trades drab courtship with an unfinished world
for a box elder bug belly up on the counter

I prefer boredom & its subtle filigree
working the ceiling into something memorable

Is it so wrong

        to go on

playing arpeggios

        to a tiny ballerina's wind-up dance

to sit around

& enumerate

the inner-life of an animal

        truculent exultations aimed at self-deflation

Prognosis: music box repels the flocks

you are you & me & him & she & Rooster's blemished
lexicon baffling myself beside myself in selfish hyperbole
you are you & he & me's a she with boy parts for a girl's
part in Rooster play affection's always publicly masked to
mistake him mistaking her instinctively tame history you
are you & me & him & she & Rooster's flushed red standing
feathers stand for outmoded chivalry yes sir I'm madam
to a hen's dogma of danger-chuckles receding like consummate
you & you are him & she & I'm stuck a fraud to think in
dignity gives Rooster back his sickly stupid gaze you are you
& me & him & she & the Rooster's aggressive wonder wanders
austere horizon hopes to say wake again with the world in
your mouth salvaging prude armor of a pride encased by lesser
speech with louder reach so go faithful straight's a human fate

You & Roo's collaborative poem
on the ills of capital
You & Roo's condemnation of nudity
with all clothes removed

Blah, blah, blah... the body, etcetera

La-la-la... Lacan, etcetera

All these poets disgusted by flowers
ashamed of the semen covering everything in sight

Blah, blah, blah—the body
La-la-la—Lacan

This bare spot where bark's abraded
is perfect for carving your name

Go ahead, throw a tantrum
Tumultuous terrible eros pierces everything

> so like a dance whose choreographer insists
> each participant know only her own part
> producing on stage the genuine surprise
> life otherwise lacks

Admissible proximity
Admissible plastic window shade

placating what's outside the apartment

Props for a new avoidance principle

Meanwhile, we played cards
horribly, marked dull clockwork
of unmeasured intrigue

    It's my fault
rummaging through dead-ends of daily experience
        capitalizes on gratuitous snowfall
            to sculpt some metonymic purity

How cold are your hens?
he asks, pacing or plotting

I don't want a protector, won't admit
a nostalgic disturbance makes a minor noise

Dear boulevard
　　scissored between
　　　　what passes by
　　　& stationary
　　accruals we call scenery
　I'll admit to having
　　　no idea where I'm headed
　　Pressure to recount
　　　　the look of the road
　　or strange allures
　　　　of an accident
　　　　　keeps gorging itself
　　　　　　fakes fluency
　　　　　in punctured turbulence
　　　　an unconsumed thing
　　　　　calls for
　　　　cultivates a poem
　　full of orange cones
　　　　　stopping zones

Redundant Theme Meter reads:

—:—:—Unabashedly Wielding Imagined Life—:—:—:—:—:—:—:—:—

Sometimes I like to put things in order
like emancipation from idyllic entanglements

      "red helicopter"

      "real halo"

      "rotten protagonist"

or simply a walk to the store made meaningful?

   It's true
escalator's going indefatigably up
   an irreducible mystique
I'd readily accord it
   claiming baggage
like everyone else
   so morning breaker
chatty cavalier
   say how you got here

First a myth about expansion & contraction

Then a classically antique butterfly-shaped soul
doubtful certainties ascribed to a child's memory
of distance & boats, indifference
contemplating indifference, a gangplanked idea
gone to the fishes, everyday speculative sedation
meant to knock us out of flowers
painted on aluminum
follow those for whom
a little amateur novelty
lets the thought percolate

All suchness & other tragedies on tracing paper

Do you like calculation?

They stuck me in a box & said you made your bed etc.

What could I steal?
The view of a manicured lawn from two flights up?

My job is just that:

pretend watcher wannabe
    courting sincerity's assembly line correlatives—
        a warehouse full of dust-filled etiquette books
            for the antiquated stance a chivalrous undertaker
                & his so sorry so sorry empathy regime
                    paints over the perfect postcard sunset
                        passing this baton of abrasive self-reflection
                            to the me follows from the you-she-he
                            I'm undeniably embedded in

Found incongruous
with expanding logic
or founded in congress
with the inability
of agreement
to solve for its own
variable constituents
a definition of jurisprudence
free from the mention of law
a dead end ending in allegory
dies in an alley obscured by snow
so the only thing I do
with the lesson of the lone gunman
is shooting my mouth off

—gored by temporal conditions
or conditioned by temporal gore—

meaning a new human absolved
of culpability & a powder blue hat
both torn from the world of contingencies
where someone's knocked
another rubbery nail in place
pace from tragic midnight
to tragic empirical joke
stabbing a fork into the yoke

Is it sonorous
    this line in the sand that says
        majestic as a new dress
        I'm not naked anymore
            than divinity is
                a ground-up group photo
                    of grade school nostalgia

Method is moment to moment
 grin to grimace
    acting out the urges
        converge into mirror image
            minor imago unconsciously idealized

Little id's leash: fully flesh tone & feathered

That don't sing
for nothing dearie O dearie!

Tried getting silk socks around those claws?

    No, I'd be a gorgeous truck driver
    egregious as any fencepost animal

Who asked you to name the presidents in order
like utility's a thing to hang from your belt loop?

Brilliant new day in its entropic decay!

I just want to press my middle parts into art

Gimme gimme pelican architecture

the shape of the forest not the forest

happy ink's unabridging machine

a bit of ivy slowing a yellow wall

Things happen in lines, windows, flakes

You pluck feathers every morning

Other people have more diamonds, bigger diamonds

Is that something Roo would wear?

A grand denial
or a horse-drawn carriage
one pictures antiquity
as one placates cognition
whose epicenter
is only a rough draft
of all the possible exits
he argues exist
something
like a blue jay
pushing past the window
an obvious way out
unwinding thinking thread
in favor of the luster
a pastoral flash elicits
what original isn't
a received idea
equals two
birds like this poem

In formation above
  one's inclement sense
    of interior weather
      neurons firing in the ditch
     make a bed for the river
   a heavy rain brings on
I'm stuck with equations
  passing like geese
    An hour of pacing
  finds a skylight
to push them through
like a human-interest story
  easing dead air over dinner's
   only the daily grind
    gone full circle
     still at a red light
    & the dog demands
   friendship graciously
not an excuse that'll
stay with you like buckshot
A bad day's account gone bright with it
Appellate rejuvenation, accelerated change
The parking lot attendant's playing holiday music

loud turbulence

a love song

Accidentally picturing
fierce consequences
there's rotten drama in a seed
adding its impoverished acoustics
to the house
as it already houses
boards it might become
& noise disappearing between them

.

Goodbye King Idiocy burning dirt

Birdthought attaching itself to air
            arrives as a terrible conclusion
All this running on irrational exuberance

    O skeletal remains of the mastodon!
    O archaic apostrophe!
What's reconstructed in our image of history's accompanying aura?
        Blue light buying a museum?
        Red light selling the farm?

An animal cry interrupts the inheritance
    of another perfectly placid pastoral
        gone flaccid on the waiting room wall
            My thing's dealing with eggs, off hours
                I claw pictures of myself into the coop
                    wait for the sun to start its scrolling—
                            a pious devotee to coherent chronology

Drama mapped a cricket
       fiddling genderless noise

    Hello Hello

       Hello Hello

    Mimetic heart means copy me

    Light falls

      or fails to sound grass

A bit of soft music
from the loud speaker
dufflebagged
in idiot rain
indoor animals

One more valley, one more hill
The intellectual thing was north

    Gray sky's
overused objective
    wants in a green bottle

      green abundance

O attitude, what grows me like this?

A parade not a moving locality

a common contradiction

not musical traffic

Brother Negation's got

a stalemate

mirroring Rooster shape

chips away

ropes, slates & pins

a simple tree

in place of a missing subject

& sound

tambourines

A bird elicits real ambient beauty
wills me a capable compulsion machine
flipping the difficulty switch, high-pitched chatter
to ward off carnivores or saying a little extra
in case it won't pass the incubation period

Unaccountable lust beginning unseasonably
strikes a chord into balcony ambiance
Better keep where it fell, a brittle lookout tower
subtle acuity of someone who'd spend the day in war paint

There's a moment inside overhauls its own loose ends
Luxuriant staples in a mauve-lined room, romantic silence
Maybe the week's non-consensual letup
Ambulance sirens coat the atmosphere around such latent arrivals
Everything by ship when it's slippage I'm after

Turning circles in crisp air
turns him predictable as a thought
wedged in the crumbled end of a week

What a machine does is work!

...bricks //   ...shoes //   ...archways

Blah, blah, blah, the body
        compelling organized paint

It's uncapsizable

So what if no chicken flies, you'll have Rooster
        to coax out an ambient "of"
every practical consequence in tow

I know for a fact

a moving sentence

goes somewhere

adopts a trajectory

adopted by doubt

wakes another flying dream

hands her an aluminum can

crushing nonsense

in the kitchen

one fashions around it

Cageyness wanting
to capture a voice
or a voices or a vow
made to order
appeasing this urge
to throw a name around
like it's immobile
& keep pecking
avows to keep
the pecking
in its place
trained to contour
an impassable chuckle
while being funny
with bloody feet
they'd for luck
boil & tether to
a deathbed bronzed
above the steeple
where below
dirt whirs
from stabbing spurs
rise in porous
man-shaped particles
electrifying womanhood
into a perfect human cup:
condensation ruining
table's veneer—
superficial smear

It takes both blue wires & red wires
charging vague wiltings
of a worn-out hour
where harvesting one's monopoly on gardenias
adds to the outlook grinder, what?

Expressivities?

To cull from a machine
something machine-like
anointing menacing rural disturbances
nestled in the belfry with rusty coping mechanisms
a kind of blatant truancy

Elsewhere

three roses

in a green pail

on an island

between passing cars

suspended

earthen

gray-backed

pink clouds

Elsewhere the problem is ubiquitous fiction

On the dash, a bottle & its baby ship

one wants to touch
tiny sails
a spider
rigged
to the glass
pick from
among dead flowers
a perfect model
for one's point

A shooting position's a shooting position

Ask, interpreter
  of oracular
pronouncements, ask
  for exuberance I won't name
your flowering hate
  a simple ego, ask how
many voices raise
  a choir, I mean this
is measuring not
  pageantry, dear sweet
silly blind Rooster
  who can walk so
inflated loving it, ask
  if accosting one's image
is dangerous, considering
  the kaleidoscope
if a still picture
  of earth is enough?

What a rooster is
    stubborn alienation
 fertile adornment
a common weather vane's
  most compatible match
steady indication
  of which way
 winds are blowing
distinctive double squawk
  muffled wing beats
   O my lord, revered priest, devotee
  brave shame brooding
all my erect ones
   how many kids
equal a kingdom
 not present
  a hen takes the role
stops laying
  & begins to crow
O my lord, revered priest, devotee
   what a rooster is
blah, blah, blah, the body

Because you's a he
—what?—nine months shy
of thirty—incubating hobbyist
knows it's a die-cast figurine
from a farm scene

Here's the closeted escape:

domestic fatalism
making rounds
in a model train wears
its new male femininity
like a hacky sack in a fanny pack

Hello conductor dancing
your self-imposed, self-serving
ouster in the attic, circle the station
every ten minutes to trace
a word from the ministry
of inside things:

new facts move on old tracks
their constituent elements
converging into
the latent wakeup call
that's alarmingly passé

—cock-a-doodle-doo!—
—cock-a-doodle-doo!—
—cock-a-doodle-doo!—
—cock-a-doodle-doo!—
—cock-a-doodle-doo!—
—cock-a-doodle-doo!—
—cock-a-doodle-doo!—
—cock-a-doodle-doo!—
—cock-a-doodle-doo!—
—cock-a-doodle-doo!—
—cock-a-doodle-doo!—
—cock-a-doodle-doo!—
—cock-a-doodle-doo!—
it's Roo's sonnet for you

Stuff his romantic notion rifling in
a new day & its transient, watchtower seismology
"Your penis-tucked-between-the-legs pose
isn't fooling anyone," says the Rooster
conspicuously to himself in my shadow
He wants me to pee on the page
to keep other people out, but
I'm not so territorial making art salute
autonomous castration, an ethics fitted for Levis
while I go on with my emergency
gluing macaroni to a paper plate
Who thinks harder wants an elastic god
to bronze the cul-de-sac
for a wage, skipping pebbles
underneath the image generator
honing in useful neglect
So just stop & listen & stop & listen
you can hear it banging out dutifully

A rack of folding chairs flares dull fluorescence
of a school-dimmed mind into the possible order
of an un-peopled, re-peopled (no steeple!) republic
atop the waning afternoon, the castled, crossed-out
Xed-over could have afternoon & its nothing brigade
its nominal, normal neo-nonconformist fist in hazy air

It's not violent to punch yourself full of opposable thumb envy
If only I didn't—if he/she didn't—have to be still to stall it—
the dripping (stalactite or stalagmite?—I forget) dipping
thought barometer affixed to this diorama of
Plato's Cave via plowed fields of a non-allegorical Animal Farm
in which the pecking order says stop all the bullying
bookstores aren't erotic, collect the eggs & be off
Yes, sometimes all a stone does is eating

A tree in his mouth's a broken telephone
where I'm always talking aren't I
willing this regression a parenthetical stickhouse
to keep warm, burning the foundation
& balking at his coterie of hatchling cinders

Remove the irony actual animals in your life inculcate

Now that's an unobtrusive command
coming from a creature insulated by its own plumage

Sorry, but coloring your nouns ain't
an erudite extrapolation of identity

    What we want is real motion
        not cluck cluck clucking machines
            cantilevered by fraudulent dexterity
              a backdrop of changing seasons
                tracing digressive moves
                  of a make-believe bird
                    brings to the single act
                        exiting Rooster stage righteously

"Sense is some-
    thing else you
make willingly"
    he or she
    or me says
    to no one
in particular

Score this dismantled

busy busy mountain

masticates dimestore largesse

Goodbye training wheels
gentle thinking jarred

I blame driveways, withered oaks
the dented shaft of a streetlamp

Weather reports

what the wind does

is ruin

Endearment
eclipsed
 by mothballing
thought bubbles
 above an auto-
biographic still
 she'd let slip
into the final cut
 a film moves
like a singing
 phone, so stop
stop ringing
 in my fear
tiny pacing
 saboteur
that's not
 a phrase—
it's an action…
 listen, of course
this is second
 hand, time
passes in the
 third person
& I am I think
 speaking
for myself

Roo, Roo, the big comma
    not dancing with you
       is teaching others to pop
    their images like we
couldn't just look
    around a still life
       assault on attention

       Adjectives
       complicate
       everything
       one carries

Guess I doubt there's
    a real fake fruit bowl
       flower bundle buried
    in any what-I'll-say-
they've-done-to-me
    lifts us from this
       henhouse skepticism
           pecking its way through
pebbles painted like feed

Watching the lake
            Roo lets go the thought
    of winter in her patchwork boat
            ransomed clarity
            taking root
    in codes, masks
flaring like money
        thinking
        if only this were expansive
manipulating ink
        all I want
        gives moral sanction
    the sole of a shoe
    faint praise of some noble obsession

Nebulous space between next week
   & that line of trees amounts to the ball-chain
my mind can't help but drag

What emerges is hope for something to sink these doctored teeth into

A divination unaccustomed to cracked walls, strips of paint
about to voice what gathers in the corner
shivers a bit, rights itself, wiping off cobwebs

How long does it take to muster that kind of attrition?

Everyone's an alien

to squalor's ghost

electromagnetic fallout

snow & its interior silence

    Calling an asset an awful thing
   wakes a cheap animal & yes
    already it's yesterday
saw a bird the big so what
   made just a word later on
siding with a rhetorical triangle
   sounding as direct
as what might warrant
   a double take for one's
initial failure to charm
   the lens into focus

Film's the only metaphor I understand anymore

The first painting
you'd ever done
is the best you'll do
not because you didn't
know what it was
that you were doing
but because you didn't
know what it was
that you weren't

Day turns on
        a labored map
of what recounting
        gets in the way of:

        a yellow jacket in a cup
        on the windowsill
        window overlooking
        a line of birches
        their shadows striping
        the railroad bridge
        shading the road below
        how it curves past
        the pale granite library
        that I've yet to color in

Rooster nudged with its beak a cigarette butt

a spot of traffic

& afternoon's assemblage is won

What happens
in the center of the canvas
constitutes attention
scavenging time
like food, food
        like water, water
        a brush—

    paint doesn't move unless you make it

Dream a stage & stand on it

Dream a page from the Book of Best Endings & claw it to confetti

Organic decay of the already-dead image
    imagination's iniquitous insurgents install
        as monarch to drive each machine
            into authority's incontinent self-importance

There's no spectacle in a dying species

Put it plainly
    says the audience shaped as an open wound
    says subjecthood's crusting matter
        matted like these feathers
            I dare not fan out
                in the face of so many
                retro-sublimity chasing
                neo-earnest supplicants
            to the anti-sexual bloating
            of a hacked-apart daisy
                reflected in a mirror
                & photographed like
                    a signature big enough
                    to blot out the sky

Part conduit, part connector, poor poor
audacious construct: we's the plainest we can be

Rain soaked, the radio
    & its routine morning
deliverance make it
    half as overwhelmed
as breakfast, but playing
    it only appeases
the other part of my
    tag-along wounds
asking if it was
    an atom, an
aphrodisiac, or
    just Eve
turned confidant
    to a quiet study
area where
    disturbing others
would be
    wasting space

Either way, these
    metronome headaches
settle radiantly
    Nothing makes
jousting more
    egregious

Someone wants
pent aggression
penning him in
I don't say this
without action
an observer's
self-indulgence
inflating optimist
tendencies
with a tentacle
in every pie
just want for once
my own meal
uncorked & kept warm
carrying on mocking
masquerading her heroic
gas-station theatrics
for the rest of your life
you get to be an adult
trying to reconstitute
the age of the egg
& worried worried
worried about brittle
vanity inflaming
neighboring secondary
notions of the right way
to walk a street unclouded
by clingy defeatist airs

Two things Roo can tell you:

Mirrors & money run
   on the same circuit

      Girl's an adverb gardening
      abstract masters love

I don't mind needing
a conductor, what I mind
is the conductor's need
when the fox finally
makes its way into the poem
or when finality comes like a fox
to the poem at last
or when the poem finally
outfoxes itself, plans unfolding
in their perfection like a recipe
followed in every golden detail
a meal one dare not touch
going from warm to frigid
in the span of a thought
followed to its outermost
only to crumble in on itself

Dinner on the train
Dinner on the terrace

My wonderful ideas getting full of themselves
My wonderful ideas, horrible statues sulking in the lazy afternoon

Sometimes
      they get frustrated & punch the walls

Sometimes
      in their frustration
           they refuse not to walk right through them

Build a fence with your little poem
& pride turns it to towering brick

Roo in the kitchen
   eating crispy wheat crackers
      & wondering what to do next

Roo on the highway
   getting grandiose & distant with technology

You don't plunge headfirst into the pool
First, you make sure someone's there to see it happen

The sorry way my
life stomped out of
the living room

taking its
elephants with it

taking its
elegance with it

Pull pin
   Hold unit upright
Aim at base of fire
   & stand back

Pull pin
   Hold unit upright
Aim at base of fire
   & stand back

Squeeze lever & sweep
   side to side

Squeeze lover & sleep
   side to side

then who's a me that the him that's she singing bashful
diction beside yourself with yourself a selfless personification
I as I & she as me & him as she ill-gotten girly machismo
unmasks Rooster reluctantly pacing a private identity
overhauling her over him who's both me & she & he
hearing perfect harmony pitched from sexual organs
you cum she cum he cum we in reverie a sum of you
& him & she & me something to add to Rooster's ledger
letting go groundless disinterest for desirous territory
marking notches makes feigning fright a come-on for
you & he who's him is she & me but you are you & me
& him & she & Rooster uneasy thinks guard duty's
a dead end ending in allegory where he's a she performing
his womanhood in manly dress to make of dawn another mess

She doesn't

believe

in the he

that she's sure

we must have

thought into

being

but believes

in the thought

being

just like us

& thinks

everything else

unnecessary

THE NEXT YEAR:
DID YOU DROP THIS WORD

I found a word
  on the floor (aunque)
    Did you drop it?
      Was it something else
      I said expecting full
  acknowledgment?
A truck disappears
  over the transom
    Another fly's
      confusion leaking
      into the light fixture
  Is that an answer?
    Did you drop it
      to augment
      the daring validity
  you were after
    when thank you
      & goodnight's
        the oral tradition
        an argument can't tell?
    Telephone takes
  participants
There's an animal

on each end of
the leash & the most
complex knots
are only adornment
from which one
might assemble
the transitory awe
it takes to justify
calling anything
without a frame
picturesque
An awful image
trailing its imagination
around like a mute
child asks if
I'm holding something
besides my own hand
Poor architect
pitiful inventor
you can be god
of your very own
library, call reference
a sham, shake a huge
finger at interlocutors
interrupters, intangible
elisions & ineffable
abstract evasive
comportment, can
even be a grove
of trees if you
carve out ground
enough to plant them

So what! Me too!
Would that a pile
of leaves were
an excuse for stomping
so thoroughly through
rhythmic decay's mess
of the day. Trumpet.
Kick drum. Snare.
Trumpet. That's a
directive not ambiguous
aversion. In an hour
I'll move my car
forward ten feet
All hail self-congratulatory
autonomy! If I had
claws. If I had paws
If I spend a month
sculpting the soft folds
of a flower's perfect
representation
then we know beauty
wants us to make
more of it, which is
not art, newspapers
or exchange, but
the role an indifferent
actor has in performative
grace. Adjectives mucking
up expression, mauling
the flower with its own
thorns. Vibrancy spills
over the view from

my apartment because
I want it to
A dog answers
to the intonation
not the name
I don't mean this
as an aphorism
where narrative
sunrise gives narrative
seasons the tune
whistled to chop
a quarter-hour
off of narrativity's
chokehold. A poem
is not a song. It's not
a pastime. It's not
a person pretending
culpability is excused
by plucking a few
heartstrings or
fantasizing radical
critique as the new chic
I love the moon
but that's not it either
For one gloriously
troublesome moment
an ant's forgotten why
it's hauling a breadcrumb
It's the moment after this
one's getting warmer
How did I hurt your ear?
You sang in it

Attention citizens
I'm not plural
Modern alienation
that isn't indifference
but abundance asks
how many decent poems
do you know
about renting DVDs?
How many original ideas
can you come up with
as another example
of urgency's inability
to mount to the wall
anything worth a look?
Are you against observation
outside removing yourself
so far nothing
remains save degrees
Dear snowfall
around a streetlamp
how radiant am
I collapsing without
a thruway to make
headway in the
way home is
a fictitious kill switch
wired to all the adieus
of actually having
somewhere to go?
Is it better to
build a machine
than to see one

dissolve gracefully?
The most substantial
thing I've done is
eating. A cop says
"What are you doing
on this corner?" I say
"Changing my life!"
Attention Citizens
I'm not plural
(you've said that already)
A poem runs the risk
of being meaningfully
a little case study
illustrating what
one can fit inside
Is it ambition blinds
our bird not wanting
a worldly thing to do
with it but better
(bitter) poems, trading
a post in the kingdom
of narcissistic vanity
for some horse feed?
Mental action's menial
task, too many removes
too much mask. Would
that Joan of Arc stood
in awe at water trickling
its tiny-cog-in-the-big-
machine reminder down
the shower drain. Would
that baby in the bathwater's

a fast acting epiphany
for anyone willing to
pull the plug on cliché
It's not that I don't
have the patience
for an image; it's that
I can't imagine one
without a jolt into
the actual world
which is who knows
how far from where
we've wound up—here
staring at ink stains
to elicit whatever it was
the window wouldn't
A century of alienation
assaulting drainage
systems. The real
history of the lyric's
what we do with our
runoff until a garbage
truck rumbling by
wakes our bird too early
with the thought
a city's everything
outside a citizen
An objective correlative
for the ethical obligation
to account for one's time
or the Latinate slurry
of a mind in a hurry?
Our cab driver calls it

corruption with flowers
refuses another poem
about them & refusal
blossoms into haywire
tightrope mystique
meeting best first thought
under revision's house arrest
rejecting fashionably
our hypotactic mess
Thus the explainer's
containment & container
I point out the window
or at the window
I point out the window
or at the window
Balmy architecture
in place of abstraction
placing us permanently
on the periphery
of the present or
presently in the
impermanence of talk
filling the hallway
as though the tentative
aggression of a hand
testing each knob
turns on its head
the metonym that's
otherwise & always
blah, blah, the body's
literary device for
the production of money

where the people
march in your poem
(good for you, let them)
The people march
in your poem, enamored
by the fat police
grown thin. The people
march in your poem
enamored by the fat
police grown thin
as the prostitutes therein
Good for you
praise the day, every
act in your poem's
a consensual exchange
Good for you
praise the day, rub
the cocks & cunts
of your poem all
over the polis, all
over the police, all
over the marching people

Is there ever a point in cultivating nostalgia? It's not something you water &
watch grow. It just happens, hits like a thought. No, that's something you build.
I guess I mean it's void of fulfillment, though even that's dubious ground &
who'd want to stand outside waiting for the day's instructions? You don't cater
to them by letting them prance around full of self-absorption. Statues know
they're statues & there's no dignity in that. One might go on & on to a fault
& still feel there's a bit of the circle one's forgotten to fill in. It's the geometry
to planning out a life & then remembering it was math that held you back in
the first place. The addition of a blanket drying on a clothesline in the sun. A
porch umbrella locked to a banister. They're not exactly the images of thinking,

but they're here in front of me, saying, Look, can't you see the shape of your own head without staring at yourself. Reflections. I'm through with reflections. It starts to amount to something, some kind of big oak door in the way of where you think you need to be & then you're back at home, in bed, regretful for never having tried the handle, if there even was one. Self-conscious as a mockingbird. That's the human point of view for you, always ascribing worth to whatever fits into its own agenda. So what if the weather tears a big hole into your expectations. Is it wrong to wait under an awning until the world gets interesting again? Is it wrong to make a list so you can have the momentary pleasure of crossing things off? Isn't pleasure, like rain, always momentary? I wonder if this is a route to getting beyond one's understanding. The worst dichotomies become the most ubiquitous affirmations. You unfold a thing to feel it I suppose, & then you might cringe or lunge under a table. The mouse probably thinks you're the abrasive one. So why don't we let more things happen instead of treating all of it like a puppet with our hand stuffed into its guts? Is this what glamorous really means? The right light revealing every stitch, that it's all an aborted attempt to try & tailor the way the background looks. I mean you're not even supposed to notice what goes on to the left or the right. It's the center that matters & there's never anything meaningful in that. Someone on the bus has his knee pressed against your own, & you know he's cognizant of it, almost saying worship me, I'm my very best emperor. I used to see the same man several times a week press himself against teenage boys on the train in Boston. Once, I saw him do it to someone in line at the grocery store. It's sad when desire is revolting. I'm better suited to smaller things, but then I'm outside the subject again. There's the immediate oddity of discovering a plaque on a pedestal in the park on a path you'd never taken before, & trying to figure out why someone had chosen this particular spot, but is it different if I'd said finding instead of discovering? My friend Marcus loves to point out moments in film when the boom mic appears at the top of the frame. I guess artifice is exciting if you don't expect it. Fireworks on an off day, which is not a metaphor. Language can be efficacious if you let it wilt a little. That's the better part of desire, to wear your own house like a turtle. Forgive neighbors. Forgive strangers. Forgive bank tellers forced into small talk. There's no significance in forming the dots into an image of your own eye, but we sure waste a lot of time in doing it. Lately, it feels like trying on what you'd never wear or planning a trip you're not going to take. Adventure is overrated. That's why I'm obliged to think art is work.

I take this
obligation
seriously
& then set
it down
with the
same care
given a
porcelain
statue one
needs move
before wiping
the table
& placing
an apple there

Call it the long afternoon made longer when one's attempt to eke from it some modicum of joy, however intangible, gives way to the internal pressure of having to produce a monument to the same effort. This is to say it's only good enough to enjoy eating that apple if the enjoyment is recorded, played back, and tinkered with so endlessly the act becomes a self-consumption, wherein one feels as though led by one's own consciousness toward the weakly-fortified core at the exact center of the self, and forced all the while to carry aloft a banner that reads: *Experience eats alive our desire to drive it toward meaning.* All day the winds rise & fall, rise & fall, & all day the words flap above you, a cruel taunting gesture, as though you, yourself, were nothing more than text beneath a poem's title, a poor elaboration of a poor adage made poorer still by want of reaching its conceit. And once there, once windows have been shuttered, doors locked, every light dimmed, once the now deserted streets at the center of this place seem in their desolation to be baring the collective teeth from each absent face in your general direction, & the banner, now beaten threadbare, trails like the softest of shackles behind you, who is to say if it was worth it, if such crossings & counter-crossings, so much chiasmic flurry, all the little fits & starts that sent you off only to call you in again at the height of pleasure, who is to say if all this babble, all these finely tuned phrases, all the words trued with a watchmaker's temperament, if all of it were worth trading for the act from which it sprang, if you wouldn't have been better off biting into the apple without the burden of accounting for how you'd later abandon the core.

RETURNING
DIMINISHMENTS

AN IMAGE OF AN ANTIQUATED
POETIC DEVICE

Clumps of pollen drift like cloud refuse through the interior of the obvious simile.

A LADDER BUILT BY MARTIN BUBER

I suppose anything hung on a wall is heightened. A real architect wants only to collapse the world. It is the lowest rung of perfect goodness.

A MAN HOLDING A BOUQUET OF LILIES

The image is disturbed from the outset. All it does is wait around for us to consume it. The auditorium is now empty. Notes rise. Days rise. I rise, expecting more authenticity from the arbitrary deployment of echoes.

ALL LEARNING IS A SORT OF LYING

to one's self repeatedly though without the luxury of repetition. It's night.
Evening has filled with the sound of passing fire trucks. Evening continues
in all cars. Thusly, birds begin to leave our island. Why hide in the thin bridge
of a rhetorical question when one might walk suspended across such a sentence?

A POEM ACQUAINTED WITH
ALL THE USUAL ARGUMENTS

A continuous blank wall, broken here & there by a colorful door,
twists free from one's sense that enclosure is everywhere the default form
the loose urban fabric of the modern would hang itself upon, as though it
were a word uttered & then entered into, a game of riddles whose origin

one might refute with the most difficult of questions: does anyone know one?

THE GLUE HOLDS THE GUTTERS IN.
THE RHETORIC'S A LOOSE-LEAF
APPRENTICE.

Cracks in the oracular self I'm splitting open, splicing states of conscious-
ness onto what? Locomotive sound wings? A burnt rabbit in the trap &
a rabid set of number laws the numb part of me knuckles up to.
Tell it to the sludge, the oil slick, the slippage ousting us from Ollie-Ollie-

oxen-free central. I've got a drawer full of keys that bend by themselves.
Magic Realism, mute narration or just plain jack-in-the-box psychosis?

SOMETHING ELSE FOR YOUR POETRY, NO?

The pleasant day resists parsing, but tragedy too discloses, deleting
provocation dressed in a paradox of renaissance drag. Through silence
the utopia cries aloud: remove all vegetation to achieve historical authenticity.
This is the great contradiction of joy. It moves by exception, for which

there are no models, save pottery shards in plexiglass suspended by pins.
What image merits an afternoon in which the colonel's idleness expands
the idea of an audience only to be deflated by ill-timed applause?

SOME INSTRUCTION
ON CELESTIAL EXCURSIONS

Before taking a position, a brief pause is in order to analyze the manner
in which one might encapsulate it. A vehicle of expression would otherwise
run idle. One is fueled by the seeming presence of vastness, folding
an ideological outfit to ensure that no wrinkles appear in tomorrow's

performance of morally instructive, mummified beliefs. Persephone pulls
a lily from the ground & Mallarmé is again in love. They toil not
neither do they spin, innocuously speaking, filtered down to such clichés
of everyday conversation as another decorative motif pouring forth like doctrine.

ALL A SYMBOL'S EVER DONE FOR US IS REDUCTIVE

You can tutor impotently observing the decline of your empire
in students crushed by obscure ambiguity, or validate on your own
the wild structure of a leafing oak. There are no other options.
Understanding is not a table. I leave the house of my own freewill

& pass into history proper. Disavowing an apostle's terrible awareness
of emerging universals, disowning inevitable recurrence, done with
what sinks in the sea, rotted by scholarship, scornful as an arrow,
I am a friend of Aristotle, but am a greater friend of undeserved grace

turning an icicle's frantic inertness into an example of ontology.

TEN WAYS TO PUT TOGETHER
AN AIRPLANE

Turn toward the undifferentiated vastness in the first of all flowers.
Turn partly in delight & partly inspired by the sick awe of rebirth.
Turn a weakness of the libido into the asset of a well-stocked garage.
Shatter utopian tendencies against the earthly ballast that anchors them.

Turn a spiritual aspiration into the ill-omened echo of a dog's far-off cry.
Turn all animals into theologians, psychotherapists, classicists, & art critics.
This theory would liken flight to a kind of castration of the intellect.
Engage in nothing on the fringe of everyday activities save that of forgetfulness.

Turn the sonnet like a saw blade upon the woodsy fixity of received form.
Launch into the air an asexual organ of reproduction. Say it: fuel equals fear.

IMPROBABLE FOR A TEAR TO DISSOLVE ON THE LAMINATED PAGE BUT IT DOES SO

,

Add to the picture an angular stroke & artificiality trumps again
the definition of the word *design*, while in silk a spider barricades herself,
extending two pedipalps, which suggest the single couplet to survive
the Sapphic present: *Beauty endures as long as there's a looker/ but goodness*

always looks beautiful. I look at you as an aerial trip over paradise. Yes,
at the cellular level we're equals, spinning & weaving in extreme fragility
a dialectic of emergence: you can spring fully armed from the head of your father
or as a larva eat through the leaf on which your egg was lain. Either way, what

turns a removal of drama from the earth into latent sexual content allowing
the tear to soak through is not stone ripped from a statue, but an animal
singing in hurried inversions without its horn: Shalom, goodnight, adieu.

IDEAS BASED ON THE MAPPING OF
ORDINARY SPACE

Turning elevation into an allegory again? Sure, clouds look like clouds
& take the shape of the limits of one's imagination, but what I can't
understand is if you think the world organizes itself around you, or if
you're content to let your raft drift toward the best looking beachfront

one might build a megalopolis upon, taking the limits of your imagination
into account, then twisting them, as though architectural forms, facades,
& embellishments might contain a clue to the conceptual sense of home,
which, if one looks at it from a mountain, becomes somehow heightened,

turning elevation into an allegory. Sure, the clouds look like clouds,
& any one might in its singularity resemble a row of welcoming bungalows.
Understand, the world will always organize itself around your thinking,
which doesn't have to be monumental. A megalopolis begins with sand.

A POEM TO BE FOLDED
INTO THE SHAPE OF A SLIPPER

A grackle has no interest in the far corner of the field to which it is
briefly pinned. Admittedly, I put it there. Another piece of architecture
giving the elements something to act upon. Dent in the windshield.
Creak in the door. Day lavishly without language. A better subject

for paint, bitter subject of presupposition. A man, rubbing together
two dimes, removes a shovelful of dirt beneath his freshly constructed
thought. Distraction: the best way of looking at anything. I have no interest
in a perfectly clear glass of water on the kitchen counter, in perfection

turning the bird into an embodiment of disturbance. Grass drying
on pavement, dying on pavement. Underneath opacity, it is difficult
to see. The Dictionary of Symbols is suspiciously free of an entry for
the aforementioned grackle. Absolved of concern, it should be observed

that a fact can't be corroborated by its bearing of the earth on its back.

PRIVILEGING AN INSTRUMENT
OF APPROACH

What matters at submicroscopic levels? What makes a garden at night
an ill-applied example of luxury? The lizard on its rock, measuring all
things by movement. Stationary sun, sun in the shape of a tulip,
effectuate wind grinding flowers, trees tangled like curtains, the lizard

& its rock—disordered sounds pulverized into music: another fragment
like a flag claiming its constituents. I regard with great awe an annotation
to the simplest aphorism. Its order allows it to grow without ambiguity.
The rocky surface of the lizard's mind alight in the stability of an atom

turns a system of thinking disguised by allegory into the ruined house
of observation. All variables are excess. Reduce the lizard to a thought,
the flag to a thread, & sun to a smear of yellow inside the flower.
The rock is already a reduction. Reduce to a footnote all description,

to an afterthought all reaction. The house can only expand with music.
Possibility allows you to leave it. Routine will return you there.

ACKNOWLEDGMENTS

Grateful acknowledgment is made to the editors of the following journals in which excerpted versions of this work first appeared: *26: a journal of poetry and poetics, Another Chicago Magazine, Art New England, Cant, Cold-Drill, Copper Nickel, Court Green, Critiphoria, Denver Quarterly, Diode, Everyday Genius, Fourteen Hills, Front Porch Journal, Homônumos* (China), *Ixnay Reader, Jacket, The Laurel Review, Lungfull!, Massachusetts Review, Matchbook, Octopus Magazine, Puerto del Sol, Trickhouse, Your Black Eye,* and *Word For / Word.* These poems were composed and revised between 2004 and 2012. "All orange blossoms have to do is act naturally" is a line from Chuck Stebelton's *Circulation Flowers* (Tougher Disguises, 2005); this poem is for Chuck and his generosity of spirit.

Thanks as well to everyone who looked at various iterations of this work: Sara, Janet, Julie, Eric, Erik, Josh, Dana, Sommer, Sara, Kevin, Travis, Monica, Andrea, Chris, Jake, Zach, Mathias, Jules, Rachel, Cathy, Tom, Chi-Chi, etc. This book is for you.

ABOUT THE AUTHOR

NOAH ELI GORDON is the co-publisher of Letter Machine Editions, an editor for *The Volta,* and an assistant professor in the MFA program in creative writing at the University of Colorado at Boulder, where he currently directs Subito Press. His recent books include *The Source* (Futurepoem Books, 2011) and *Novel Pictorial Noise* (Harper Perennial, 2007). His essays, reviews, creative nonfiction, criticism, and poetry appear widely, including journals such as *Bookforum, Seneca Review, Boston Review, Fence, Hambone,* and in the anthologies *Postmodern American Poetry* (W.W. Norton & Co., 2013), *A Broken Thing: Poets on the Line* (University of Iowa Press, 2011), *Against Expression: An Anthology of Conceptual Writing* (Northwestern University Press, 2011), *Poets on Teaching* (University of Iowa Press, 2010), and *Burning Interiors: David Shapiro's Poetry and Poetics* (Fairleigh Dickinson University Press, 2007). An advocate of small press culture, he penned a column for five years on chapbooks for *Rain Taxi: review of books,* ran Braincase Press, and was a founding editor of the little magazine *Baffling Combustions.* He lives in Denver with Sommer Browning and their daughter Georgia.

AHSAHTA PRESS

SAWTOOTH POETRY PRIZE SERIES

2002: Aaron McCollough, *Welkin* (Brenda Hillman, judge)

2003: Graham Foust, *Leave the Room to Itself* (Joe Wenderoth, judge)

2004: Noah Eli Gordon, *The Area of Sound Called the Subtone* (Claudia Rankine, judge)

2005: Karla Kelsey, *Knowledge, Forms, The Aviary* (Carolyn Forché, judge)

2006: Paige Ackerson-Kiely, *In No One's Land* (D. A. Powell, judge)

2007: Rusty Morrison, *the true keeps calm biding its story* (Peter Gizzi, judge)

2008: Barbara Maloutas, *the whole Marie* (C. D. Wright, judge)

2009: Julie Carr, *100 Notes on Violence* (Rae Armantrout, judge)

2010: James Meetze, *Dayglo* (Terrance Hayes, judge)

2011: Karen Rigby, *Chinoiserie* (Paul Hoover, judge)

2012: T. Zachary Cotler, *Sonnets to the Humans* (Heather McHugh, judge)

AHSAHTA PRESS

NEW SERIES

This book is set in Apollo MT type
with Bauer Bodoni titles
by Ahsahta Press at Boise State University.
Cover design by HR Hegnauer.
Book design by Janet Holmes.
Printed in Canada.

AHSAHTA PRESS

2013

JANET HOLMES, DIRECTOR

CHRISTOPHER CARUSO	MELISSA HUGHES, *intern*
JODI CHILSON	TORIN JENSEN
KYLE CRAWFORD	ANNIE KNOWLES
CHARLES GABEL	STEPHA PETERS
JESSICA HAMBLETON, *intern*	JULIE STRAND
RYAN HOLMAN	ZACH VESPER